Ultimate
Signspotting

Introduction.

Seeing a funny sign in **'in the wild'** is a bit like seeing a rainbow. You don't find them as much as they find you.

Still, there's a certain amount of alertness involved. Just as you have to remember to walk outside and look up just after a rain shower passes if you want to catch a rainbow, you need to look a little longer at signs you'd otherwise ignore.

Drivers only recall about 20 percent of the signs they glance at. And the more often they drive by them, the more likely they are to ignore them. This is why travel is a perfect fit for **Signspotting**. We're on foot, carrying cameras, and in a new environment that demands our attention -- the trifecta of funny sign discovery.

Over the last 20 years, I've gathered well over 50,000 sign photos from well-traveled amateur and professional photographers. Trying to decide which is **unintentionally funny** enough to merit inclusion in a Signspotting book has been a challenge. Trying to select favorites among those for this 'ultimate collection' has been downright unnerving.

Just when I think I've seen every **awkwardly compromised** stick figure, bizarre warning, or confounding place name, a new one comes along. That is, new hilarious signs are going up all the time. At times, it seems like a race between the people who put up these ridiculous signs and those who try to photograph them.

Perhaps the most important thing to keep in mind as you flip through this book is that we English speakers put up more **inadvertently funny signs** than anyone else. We need very little help in mangling the English language. Now just imagine if we tried to be as kind to other nations as they are to us and put helpful signs up in Arabic, Japanese, French, Spanish, and other languages. We'd have these foreigners rolling in our streets with laughter. We'd jumpstart an entire industry of funny sign books in other countries.

So, as we enjoy these gaffes, let us do so with a dose of humility.

Doug Lansky

04

The Author.

Doug Lansky spent ten years traveling the planet, during which time he visited 120 countries (if you count San Marino). He has written a syndicated newspaper travel column, penned several books, hosted a Discovery Channel show, and delivered his funny presentation on travel around the world. He has moved his base camp numerous times, and is now living in Sweden where he has "the ultimate Ikea kit": a Swedish wife and three daughters. Doug started collecting funny signs during the first year of his travels, and it has turned into a disturbingly addictive habit.

I dedicate this book to all the alert signspotters
around the world who were smart enough to take these
photos and kind enough to send them in to me.

Are the authorities referring to the weight of the hikers or deer migration in the area?
Photo location: Colorado, USA by John R. Liboky

Little optimistic on the range?
Near Tokyo, Japan *by K McKay*

There was a time back in primary school when most of us would have gladly paid $5.99 to not get a wedgie.
Oakmont, Pennsylvania, Usa *by Cel Est E Janosko*

Your fifteen minutes starts right now

Glamis, California, USA by Mary Stampone

灌木林步行徑

若非與經驗步行者同行，
請勿步過警告牌。

등산길 경고문

등산에 관한 전문지식이나 경험이 적으신
분들은 이 표지판 뒤로 넘어가지말아 주시길
바랍니다.

ブッシュ・ウォーキング(山歩き)
コース

ブッシュ・ウォーキング(山歩き)の熟練者
以外は、これより先には 行かないで
下さい。

THIS SIGN IS TO PREVENT FOREIGN
TOURISTS FROM GETTING LOST

Finally, helpful tourist information.

China by Jeff Coe

Table Mountain National Park

Warning
Please look under
your vehicles
for penguins

Sponsored by
Boulders
Beach
Lodge

*The diagram in the lower left looks more like the penguins are simply
providing a free brake inspection, or maybe changing the oil.*
Boulders Beach, South Africa *by Scott Snyder*

Don't settle for second best.
Dublin, Ireland *by Allie Ono*

Safety railing for large groundhogs.
Newbiggin-by-the-Sea, UK *by Alastair Speight*

Don't worry...
it tastes like chicken.
Ontario, Canada *by Jonah*

But you may cling to the outside.
Derby, England *by Richard Still*

Too much yeast?
Norway by Doug Lanksy

a mael

焼おにぎり：A burning condition rice ball · · · · · · · · · ·

おにぎり：A rice ball · · · · · · · · ·

卵 ゞ 炊：Egg porridge of rice and vegetables · · · · · · ·

り茶漬け：Paste boiled rice in tea · · · · · · · · ·

梅茶漬け：A lower prostitute is soaked · · · · · · · · ·

鶏 雑 炊：Bird porridge of rice and vegetables · · · · · · ·

鮭茶漬け：Salmon boiled rice in tea · · · · · · · · ·

明太茶漬け：Dried pollack dried cod boiled rice in tea · · ·

Appetizers

You might try the soaked prostitute.
Kyoto, Japan by M. Rosenlund

'Alternative fuel' or even *'natural gas'* might be more appropriate.

CAUTION

DO NOT
DRINK WATER

FISH CRAP IN IT

*Do not drink water would
have been sufficient.*
Camrose Alberta Canada *by Marliss Taylor*

Enjoy the Cemetery.
Please keep Rover
on the leash!
(psst: it's the law)

*How about an elephant
on a leash?*
Vancouver, BC *by Félix Houle*

*I remember signs that told
you something useful.*
Door County WI by Harold Henckel

How does one get on the authorized animals list?
Jacksonville Zoo, FL *by Pat Cosgrove*

*All traffic will be temporarily
rerouted through Mecca.*

Olympic Peninsula, Washington, USA *by Ted Johnson*

Sailors only please.

Puerto Vallarta, Mexico by Bob Dole

Please! Don't to loss things or broken in room by guesthouse charge you.

DON'T SMOKING

YOU CAN SMOKE TO OUTSIDE.

2008 01 27

Contender for highest ratio of grammar error per word.
Phuket, Thailand *by Linda Nygren*

In other words, there's no avoiding highway 277.
Eagle Pass, Texas *by Lowell G. McManus*

flowers or fruits, no climbing trees, threatening or hurting the birds, etc.

2 Maintain the pubic sanitation, please don`t spit or relieve nature everywhere. Please put your dog-ends, vastepaper pericarp and so on into the ustbins.

 Take good care of the public establish-nent, never climb, lie or draw on the oriettes, chairs and fences.

And finally, point 5: 'Don't do drugs while you write pubic signs.'
Zhuhai, China *by Pierre Cuerrier*

That famous Nevada desert humor.
Las Vegas, NV USA *by Donna Washburne*

COMPLAINTS
ABOUT ELEPHANTS
TO BE MADE HERE
TOURIST OFFICE, AMBER Ph.530264

Tusks too long? Ears flopping about? Not taking corners so well?
We understand your elephant problems and we're here to help.

Jaipur, India by Nancy Adolphson

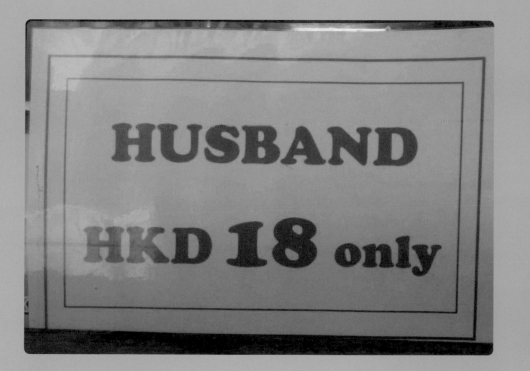

HUSBAND

HKD 18 only

May seem like a bargain, but wait until you get to know him.
Hong Kong by Helen Bin

*Why would you expect to be able
to run around here?*
Broughton, NC *by Nick Jones*

*Short circuiting sponsored
by Viagra.*
Brighton, Canada *by Richard Hill*

Murphy's law applies to signs as well.
Steelpoort, South Africa by Melvin Ekandjo

*Mmmm... haven't had a taste
of that for a while.*
North Island, New Zealand *by Daniel Oshop*

*Imagine the bedlam that would
ensue without this sign.*
Calgary, AB, Canada *by Jason Demers*

You'll just have to try the door and find out.
Woodsketch, Victoria, Australia by Andrew Fitzgerald

FOR ASSISTANCE
PUSH 3 INCH
HELP BUTTON

Do not push the 2.5 inch help button.
Berkeley Springs, WV, USA by Parker Sulivan

Just in case you forgot your shopping list.
Brooklyn, NY *by Mort Trainer*

Daydreamers beware!
Osaka, Japan *by Eden Palmer*

Now if it was worms and orange juice, that would be another story.
Wilmington, North Carolina, USA *by Jerry Harster*

Tourists have probably been wondering what all that yellowish grainy stuff is that they've been driving through for hours.

Southwest Namibia *by Nathan Broom*

34

Natural Burial and Cremation
BY WILLWERSCHEID WEST-HEIGHTS

Donate
Your Old

Dead is better, but will take old.
Where: W St. Paul, MN by *Pat Hinderscheid*

Drunken people crossing

Yes, this is an official sign. The traffic safety board felt
the need to warn drivers about tourists too drunk to stand.
Phuket, Thailand by Linda Nygren

Bedwetters welcome.
Kochin, Kerala, India by Nick Griffin

Hopefully you've got enough gas, food, and water to see you through.
Cambridge, MA, USA *by Jessica Tanny*

Well, then, perhaps you'd be kind enough to tell us what it is.
Creve Couer, MO, USA *by Dave Adams*

Liven up your next holiday season!
Green Bay, WI, USA *by Peg Zenko*

In Korea, this is what constitutes biting social commentary for the bathroom.
Seoul, South Korea *by Katja Shaye*

Should I stay or should I go now?
Monroe Vil LE, Pennsylvania, Usa *by Mari E Hammer*

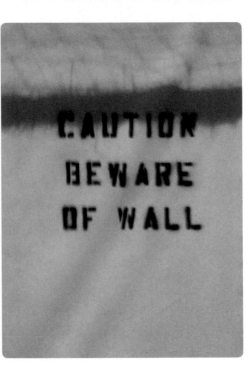

Thanks for the hot tip.
Wixom, MI, USA by Jake Leslie

*Now hold on partner, I'm afraid your car
didn't come to a complete whoa.*
Eddy's Corner by James C Esther

On the bright side, at least it's not a question mark.
Abu Dhabi, United Arab Emirates by Vince Stephenson

'Help! I have a porking emergency'
Beijing, China *by Don Thornton*

Bad dog!
Salt Spring Island, BC, Canada *by Ruth Chernia*

FREE POO
CONDITIONS APPLY

Your lucky day.
Palmerston North, New Zealand by Phillip Newport

CAUTION
WATCH OUT FOR
FALLING
CANNONBALLS

And you thought coconuts were dangerous.
Honolulu, Hawaii by Phyllis M Grosz

Ah, but of clouse.
Phuket, Thailand *by Tim Olivett*

Hey Mom, guess what? I'm living the dream.
Venice beach, California, USA *by Kathy Ramirez*

SLOW HUMP

X-rated road or lost hat area... you decide.
Bridgetown, Barbados *by Ron Flatter*

If you like bedshits, you've come to the right place.
Philippines *by MK Uy*

CAUTION

PEDESTRIANS MUST
ADHERE TO
TRAFFIC PERSONNEL

*All those pedestrians not clinging to traffic
personnel will be ticketed.*
Toronto, Canada by Ruth Cheenne

Please keep
an eye on
your children..

..otherwise we'll be
forced to send them
home with a puppy
and a double latte.

Thanks! -The Management

I believe the U.N. defines this as torture.
Oregon City, Oregon *by Vicky Enriquez*

McDonald's

BILLIONS AND BILLIONS SERVED

TRY PREMUIMM CWRAP

Freudian slip or truth in advertising?
Decatur. Georgia *by Diana Snyder*

Chewing Gum

Visitors to the Jewel House are earnestly requested not to discard chewing gum on the floors, nor to dispose of it on showcases and doors.

Gum chewers unite. This little 'chew in' was staged at the entrance to London's Crown Jewels exhibit.

London, England *by David Kennedy*

DO NOT FEED THE ELEPHANTS, IT CREATES MANAGEMENT PROBLEMS

Executives battle over elephant feeding.
Johannesburg Zoo, South Africa by *Nicki Gilbert*

*In other words, we have lots of guns and
we're looking for target practice.*
Moorcroft, WY *by Joshua Lund I*

The Sunshine House®
*A Tradition
in Early
Education*

www.sunshinehouse.com

WE PROVIDE FREE
ASS

1208

Now that's an offer!
Matthews, NC *by Kelley Hyatt*

This is how the goat is going to take you down. Don't say we didn't warn you.
Nara, Japan *by Evi Sickinger*

부드러운 게 튀김

Fried soft Crap

The fried crab is also nice.
Seoul, South Korea by Heather Augar

WARNING
TO TOURISTS
DO NOT LAUGH
AT THE NATIVES

Discreet snickering OK.
Pocatello, Idaho, USA, by Maureen Winter

Under normal conditions, of course, all aircraft would come to a compete stop when passing over a stop sign.
Payson, Arizona, USA *by Kenneth Adamec*

This one doesn't count.
Wiscasset, Maine *by Sarah Meisel*

From the department of contradictory emergency information.

Holland Village, Singapore by Matthew Warren

439-1250

SEPTIC TANKS PUMPED
SWIMMING POOLS FILLED
NOT SAME TRUCK
439-1250

Thanks for clarifying.
Bismarck, ND *by Brian Palmer*

I think I can hold it.
Benodet, France *by Patricia Floc'h-Anderson*

You're on your own. Good luck!

Golden Gate Bridge, San Francisco, California, USA *by Cristen Rene Andrews*

The 255,026 km² state will presumably reopen after renovations.

Klamath Falls, Oregon, USA *by April Gray*

STARLIGHT
GOURMET COFFEE

喜来特咖啡

밀크커피　Milk Coffee

연한커피　Tasteless Coffee

진한커피　Strong Coffee

Now with less taste than ever.
Location: Beijing, China *by Sterling Bell*

花草皆有生命
Flowers and plants have life

敬请用心呵护
Please caress attentively

南洋博仕欣居小区
Nanyang bo shi xin living area

We don't want to get in the way of your
horticultural fondling, but just go a bit easy.
Shanghai *by Yi-Ling Bauchau*

New niche market in massage.

York City, England *by Trevor Warren*

DISCHARGING FIREARMS ILLEGAL

Clark County Code 12.04.230

*Nice to see reverse psychology is
so effective with gun owners.*
Las Vegas, NV *by Jay Aldrich*

PLEASE HELP KEEP BOOGERTOWN CLEAN

Giant tissue, anyone?
Pigeon Forge, Tennessee, USA *by Jeri Phillips*

EXIT 329 CLOSED
SUCKS TO BE YOU BUT
I GOT FIRED TODAY SO
DONT EXPECT ANY HELP

Hard to blame him.
Wyoming *by Jonah*

*Either an odd way to prevent tourists
from boarding or it's the transport
for a losing team's road trip.*
Skagway, Alaska, USA *by Erik Lange*

Hey blind people, look here!
Australia *by Dan Dowling*

Unless you have a miracle up your sleeve, you might
wait until winter before attempting this.
Glendaloch, Ireland *by Karla Richards*

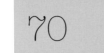

DOGS - PLEASE SHUT THE GATE

It's just a matter of fine breeding and proper education.
Henley-on-Thames, England *by Margo Scafield*

ANYONE. CAUGHT. SHOPLIFTER WILL
BE SHOT 100 TIMES THE VALUE OF THE
STOLEN ITEM (S)

ขโมยสินค้าปรับ 100 เท่า

In other words, steal some chewing gum and your body gets more holes than a sponge.
Amazing that there's a single Thai word for all that.
Ko Samui, Thailand *by Edward Skupien*

SÚPER ARMPIT WHITENING

SATISFACTION GUARANTEED!!!

Wow, your sparkling white armpits look fantastic!
Flushing, New York, USA by Young Whan Choi

What'll it be, filet meow or hot dog?

Port Townsend, Australia by Alexandra Watkins

You're not going to believe this, but see that big hill in front of you? Well, it's blocking the view of what's on the other side. No, seriously. It is.

Richfield, Wisconsin, USA by Keith Noppen

The emperor's new fence.
Pine Township, Pennsylvania, USA *by Ken and Tricia Sutton*

Did you ever wonder what life would be like if they let lawyers write street signs?
Florida, USA *by Michelle Prettitore*

*There's something over there,
but we're not sure what it is.*
Zemah, Israel *by Tord Nyberg*

*Now here's a challenge for even the
most experienced traveller...*
Namibia *by Einar Rossaak*

It's hard to read the text beneath 'Clearview'. Maybe it says 'of this bush' or 'in the other direction'.
New Hampshire, USA *by Jay Bohlen*

PORN LAUNDRY

พร ชัก อบ รีด

Filth cleaned here.
Pattaya, Thailand by David Rider

Business is booming.
Cairns, Australia *by Ralph Samuelson*

CAUTION PEDESTRIANS WALKING

Perhaps only in Michigan, America's automotive heartland, do people need to be reminded that pedestrians may actually be on foot.

Rocks National Lakeshore, Michigan, USA *by Shirley Reeve*

Parking Pac-Man.

Waimea Shopping Center, Big Island of Hawaii, USA *by Kimberley Ambrose*

Keep your hands away from the cages. You may be clawed, bitten or covered in drool.

Isle of Eriska, Scotland *by Anne Buckingham*

If you can read this, either you're driving too high or flying too low.
Maui, Hawaii, USA *by Robert Hawley*

If you see rain or snow, take shelter immediately.
Grass Valley, California, USA *by Ernie Sowell*

Please do not Annoy, Torment, Pester, Molest, Wor
Badger Harry, Harass, Hackle, Persecute, Irk, Rag
ex, Bother, Tease, Nettle, Tantalise or Ruffle the Ani

डावू , अस्वस्थ, झुलवू , निराश, हाल, व्याकूळ करू नका दुःख, त्रास,
डिवचू , छळू , मारू, हेळसांड, चिडवू नका. क्षुब्ध करू नका.
ाट, आवाज टाळा. हुसकू नका. हल्ला करू नका. मारू नका. उपद्रव देऊ
सताऊ नका यातना वेदना देऊ नका. पिडा, छेडू , खोड्या काढू नका.

Microsoft Word synonym generator
seems to be working.

注意安全!
TAKE CARE!

小 心 落 水!
FALL INTO WATER CAREFULLY!

Uncontrolled falling will be penalized.
Black Dragon Pool Park, Lijiang, China *by Robert Oaks*

Who knew safety was such a high-risk activity?
Suzhou, China *by Matthew Cockburn*

*Well, the parishioners have
been duly warned.*
Vermont, USA *by Marc Christofferson*

OK, we get it.
Gresham, Oregon, USA *by Mike Durrell*

Further up, it turns into Hilarious Valley Trail.
Apache Junction, Arizona, USA *by Mike Brown*

88

COUNTY ISLANDS

Swindon Centre

Cirencester
A 345
(A 419)

Wroughton
Devizes
(A 361)

Welcome to roundabout hell.
Swindon, UK by Harry Chamberlain

Please! Don't to loss things or broken in room by guesthouse charge you.

DON'T SMOKING

YOU CAN SMOKE TO OUTSIDE.

Receiving you loud and clear.
Phuket, Thailand *by Linda Nygren*

As is typically the case in most parts of Switzerland, just beware of the giant skeleton that will grab your car.
Switzerland *by David Gillett*

After you pick one out, swing by my place. I've got some swamp land in Mozambique to sell.

Rome, Georgia, USA *by John Tauxe*

台大開業醫師的服務

YELLING DENTAL CLINIC

一流的設備 誠摯的服務

Maybe they could be more liberal with the painkiller.
Taipei, Taiwan *by Jim Solinski*

You never know when invisibility is going to strike.
Near Ngorongoro Crater, Tanzania by Josh Kaplan

AVOID

SLEEPING NEAR THE WINDOWS,
WEARING HEAVY JEWELS, LEAVING
THE LUGGAGES AS ABANDONED,
FRIENDSHIP WITH STRANGERS,
VICTIMS OF SPURIOUS DRINKS,
BE ALERT THROUGHOUT THE JOURNEY.

Have a pleasant journey.

Do you suppose this would include the
annual trip to visit the in-laws?
Moline, Illinois, USA *by Jean Olmstead*

Well, you can't blame them
for calling it as they see it.
Lhasa, Tibet *by Gene McCullough*

When life imitates a Far Side cartoon.
White Sands National Monument, New Mexico, USA by *John Voll*

The warning every store needs.
Mendocino, California *by Andrea Ventris*

公众场所，
贵重物品妥善保管！

Please take care of your values!

Philosophical crimes ahead.
Guangdong, China *by Ava DeMarco*

What happened to equal-opportunity pain inflictors? Sue the bastards.
Warwick Castle, England *Photo credit: Hollis Tischner*

Most minefields forbid entry It's OK to enter this one as long as you reduce speed.
Near Stanely, Falkland Islands *by Tony Wheeler*

*How the local police department plans
to finance their next party*
Nichol Asvill E, Kentucky, USA *by John Wareham*

当心滑跌
DON'T FALL DOWN

Fallen pedestrians will be fined.
Forbidden City, Beijing, China by Silje Thoresen

残疾人洗手间
DEFORMED MAN TOILET

I'm not quite sure what to make of this.
Shanghai, China by Johnny Kuo

Bottomless Pit
65 feet deep

OK, nearly bottomless.
Maui, Hawaii, USA *by Scott Mason*

NOTICE

THIS BRIDGE IS RATED FOR A
MAXIMUM OF 11 TONS
ELEPHANTS ARE THEREFORE
REQUESTED TO CROSS TWO AT A TIME ONLY

Elephants take note.
Sweetwaters Game Preserve, Kenya *by Marie Guzman*

PORKY CHILDRENS WEAR

키아동ᄇ

Cleverly avoiding the word 'fat'.
Seoul, South Korea by Sean Madison

*Perhaps it's part of a helpful driving-tip series: 'sit up'
and 'keep breathing' signs are up ahead.*
Arizona, USA *by Ann Richards*

Finally, a cemetery for those who want to have the last laugh.

New Brunswick, Canada *by Rosie Barber*

Toad Suck Park NEXT RIGHT

According to local legend, this park (yes, it is an actual park) was a popular spot for bargemen to drink rum. They are said to have "sucked on bottles until they swelled up like toads." Now there's an image worthy of commemoration.

Near Little Rock, Arkansas, USA by Murray Leibowitz

It's pronounced just as it looks.
Aswan, Egypt by Dr Jos Stratford

Hey kids, forget the amusement park – it's open-house fun day at the funeral home! Last one in the car is a rotting corpse.

St. Petersburg, Florida, USA *by Jeanne Keith*

It's hard to blame them. Have you smelt travelers' feet lately?

Entrance to a temple, Yangon, Myanmar *by Gina Flaharty*

Join now and we'll have you looking pathetic in no time!

Nothing captures the spirit of Easter like a little handgun action. Reserve your firearm now for next Easter so you don't miss out on the fun.

Racine, Wisconsin, USA by Jenny Rice

Stay back... that seagull will mess you up.
Point Lomas, San Diego, CA *by Jack Clor*

Brand new antiques!
Los Angeles, California, USA *by Emmanuel Tissot*

And I, I chose the path less traveled by.
Nafplion, Greece *by John Jaeger*

ALL TREE

🙌 Thrift Store

PSYCHIC

Prophesy: "I predict you will save thirty percent on a pair of used jeans."

Temecula, California, USA by Saul D Feldman

BIG FOOT XING

DUE TO SIGHTINGS
IN THE AREA OF A
CREATURE RESEMBLING
"BIG FOOT" THIS SIGN
HAS BEEN POSTED
FOR YOUR SAFETY

Don't worry, it's only Sasquatch.
Pikes Peak Highway, Colorado, USA by John Yang

*Paradise found: only 12km, mind
the "no exit" warning.*
Between Glenorchy and Paradise, New Zealand *by Jon Morrow*

There's nothing like a few hunters roaming the premises to help drum up some business. Maybe they should change the name of the hospital to "Almost Safe Haven."

Mitchell, South Dakota, USA *by William Cumming*

BEWARE OF BABOONS & MONKEYS!
- KEEP ALL FOOD STUFF LOCKED AWAY
- CLOSE THE POP-UP ROOF OF THE CARAVAN
- REPORT ANY BABOON ACTIVITY IN THE CAM
TO THE BABOON HOTLINE (082 802 1201)

HAVE A PLEASANT STAY

*Good morning, baboon hotline,
how can I help you today?*
Kruger National Park, South Africa by Sherry Yamamoto

此博物馆每日消毒

Our Museum is disinfected
Every day

Sanitized for your protection.
Location: Shanghai, China *by Drew Strellis*

Pssst, don't tell anyone.
Darwin, Australia by Andrew Bain

Hey, I hooked a feisty one.
Twain Harte, California, USA *by Ralph Breyman*

This is one content cleric.
Ambridge, Pennsylvania, USA *by Dan Sadler*

The minibar of this hotel is stocked with a full selection of antihistamines.
Singapore by Roberta Netten

Pssst. Can you keep a secret?
Essex, England by Phil Crane

PIQUE NIQUE
PIC NIC AREA
PICK NICK PLATZ
AREA DE PIC NIC
AREA PER EL PIC NIC

It looks like a team of translators was brought in for this task. Or maybe it was just one guy making them up. In which case, he forgot "el picko nicko" and "piazza del pica nica."

Château de Chenonceau, France *by Katie Miller*

We know a street when we see one.
Lake Geneva, Wisconsin, USA *by Mike Franzene*

DEAD
PEOPLES
THINGS
FOR SALE

*Have you ever wondered what you'd get if you
combined a funeral parlor and a flea market?*
Brunswick, Georgia, USA *by Judy Richards*

FOR SALE

You can't say they didn't warn you.
Japan by Rod Heft

ZONA ARQUEOLÓGICA DE
MONTE ALBÁN
O A X A C A

¡Cuidado! El agua de los baños no es para beber y por favor...

¡No la desperdicie!

Warning! Water for the toilet is not drinkable

Well, gee, normally drinking out of the toilet in Mexico is just fine.
Hard to imagine what the problem might be in this instance.

THIS ENCLOSURE SPONSORED BY FREE THE BEARS FUND INC.

www.freethebears.org.au

Sadly, the irony is lost on the bears.

Photo by Diana Barber

Now that should put tourists at ease.
Krabi, Thailand *by Anna San Valentin*

Some Kind of Fish from The Red Sea

This photo was taken in the Alexandria Aquarium, or as the employees there like to call it: "Some kind of place that keeps fish in tanks."
Alexandria, Egypt *by Jeff Vize*

CAUTION

Please be aware that the balcony is not on ground level.

Caution: hotel management thinks you're stupid.
Austin, Texas, USA *by John Zachar*

Hey, it's Southern California. You don't break a sweat until you have to.
San Diego, California, USA *by William Brown*

Unlimited Happy Meals, eternal French fries, and not a word about cholesterol. What more could the dearly departed want?

Marksville, Pennsylvania, USA by David Cobb

AVES
Wisconsin's Finest
TAXIDERMY & CHEESE

Here's an interesting business model: lure them in with the animal mounting, then sell them cheese. Presumably, the cheese is incredibly lifelike.
Wisconsin, USA by *Steven Stezek*

*In theory, they should take away only your money here. And the
only thing that is inflated is the exchange rate.*

Cancun, Mexico by Jami Nhelsonic

You decide: is this sign giving instructions on how to get on an uncomfortable chairlift or is it a promotion for a ski-in/ski-out medical clinic?

Chamonix, France *by Belinda Hillard*

Here's a reflection on Western society: we even have parking spots for people who have made a conscious decision not to park.

Burleigh, Wisconsin, USA *by William Kucharski*

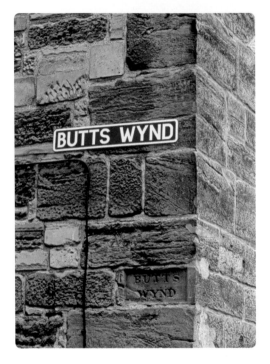

Finally an explanation for the unusually stiff
breezes that frequent this golfing mecca.
St Andrews, Scotland *by Doug Lansky*

"Welcome to Ethel" might have been
more appropriate.
Ethel, Washington, USA *by Ward Thompson*

Squied

63 The squied steams the lemon — 200
ปลาหมึกนึ่งมะนาว

64 The squied dips powder fried — 200
ปลาหมึกชุบแป้งทอด

65 The squied fried the garlic — 200
ปลาหมึกทอดกระเทียม

66 The squied cooks whore dust — 200
ปลาหมึกผัดผงกะหรี่

ปลาหมึกผัดไข่เค็ม — 200

From the new book: Thai Cooking with Dust.
Hua Hin, Thailand *by Richard Bryan*

It's about time someone put these two signs together.

Sacramento, California, USA *by Noel Bertelson*

Locals are anxiously awaiting the new "Permanent Sign".

Dublin, Ireland *by Russel Poniewaz*

Translating is clearly prohibited at the Karlstejn Castle. Or, as the sign says in Czech just above the English, 'Translating Prohibited'.

Prague, Czech Republic *by Joel M Chusid*

It's nice to see that cutting edge technology is helping to take the confusion out of sign reading.
San Luis Obispo, California, USA *by Larry Kavanaugh*

Here's one theory: maybe 'Three Mile Village' was already taken.
Kanab, Utah, USA by Carole McLaughlin

浪漫高級時鐘賓館
ROMANCE HIGH CLASS HOTEL

Why not just call it "Five-Star-Ultra-Chic-Spa-Hotel-and-Golf-Club-Rated-Number-One-By-Condé Nast Traveller" Hotel?

Hong Kong, China *by Bob Ecker*

小草有生命，
　　请脚下留情！

I like your smile,
but unlike you put your
shoes on my face.

In Chinese, it makes perfect sense.
Yunnan Province, China *by Karen Boswell*

Welcome to the traffic light from hell. At least it lets you know where you stand…or sit, idling in park, forever.

Fort Walton Beach, Florida, USA *by Richard Gaebler*

Say it five times fast.
Kuala Lumpur, Malaysia by Jason Barbacovi

It looks like those clever canines will have to confine their play to dog-friendly courses.
Sierra College Campus, California, USA *by Pat Lucas*

Apparently, there's no fine for flagrant grammatical violations.
Badaling, China *by Rosann McCullough*

Despite some progress in the 1970s, it seems hippies are still second-class citizens.
Madison, WI, USA *by Russ Kranz*

IF DOOR DOES NOT OPEN DO NOT ENTER

This is what happens when fortune-cookie writers are forced to seek employment elsewhere.

Neenah, Wisconsin, USA *by Sue Bayer-Jabb*

New Orleans has evidently instituted some strict new laws for Mardi Gras.

New Orleans, Louisiana, USA *by Richard Bradford*

Just add a little water and those Bay Area pedestrians start slipping right out of your hands.

San Francisco, California, USA *by Alan Casamajor*

ประเข้มืน

CHOCOLATE COVERED
CROCODILE

褐乳色鳄鱼

They taste just like chicken... covered in chocolate.
Bangkok, Thailand by Renata Rhodes

'Hi. I'm looking for representation. I just drove
into a sign and hurt my neck.'
San Rafael, California, USA *by Diana Singer*

Copyright.

Published in November 2014 by Lonely Planet Publications Pty Ltd

ABN 36 005 607 983

www.lonelyplanet.com

ISBN 978 1 74360 462 5

© Doug Lansky 2014

© Photographs as indicated 2014

Printed in China
Publishing Director Piers Pickard
Commissioning Editor Jessica Cole
Art Direction & Design Dan Tucker
Layout Designer Wendy Wright
Illustrator Crush
Pre-press production Ryan Evans
Print production Larissa Frost
Front cover photo by Ted Johnson

Lonely Planet offices
AUSTRALIA
90 Maribyrnong St, Footscray,
Victoria, 3011, Australia
Phone 03 8379 8000
Email talk2us@lonelyplanet.com.au

USA
150 Linden St, Oakland, CA 94607
Phone 510 250 6400 Email info@lonelyplanet.com

UNITED KINGDOM
Media Centre, 201 Wood Lane, London W12 7TQ
Phone 020 8433 1333 Email go@lonelyplanet.co.uk